Want for Lion

Want for Lion by Paige Taggart
Published by Trembling Pillow Press
New Orleans, LA
ISBN-13: 978-0-9887257-5-1
Copyright © 2014 by Paige Taggart

All Rights Reserved. No part of this book may be reproduced in any form without permission from the publisher with the exception of brief passages cited or for educational purposes. Reproduction for commercial use is prohibited except by permission of the author.

Typesetting and Design: Megan Burns
Author Photo: Sampson Starkweather
Cover Design: Unsinkable Design

Trembling
Pillow
PRESS

Want for Lion

by
Paige Taggart

Contents :::

Your Wing Deck is a Lazy Beetle ... |9

1. Island Scenarios ... |11

   Split and Raise Force-Field on Deck ... |13
   ^^ ... |14
   Rage Without Meaning ... |15
   ^^ ... |16
   Blanket the Storm ... |17
   ^^ ... |19
   Is Land ... |20
   If Land Then Magic ... |22
   Braved The Sea ... |24
   Whose Land Is Whose ... |25
   On Sand ... |26

II. Get Your Slip On ... |27

III. Smothered In Emu Milk ... |47

IV. Starts in Herds ... |71

V. Entropy Poems ... |83

VI. To Talk Its Way Out of Me ... |89

VII. A Theory of Feathers and Warrior Gear ... |97

   Not For June ... |99
   Intergalactic Battles ... |100
   (   ) ... |101
   The Yellow Crocus of Down Under ... |102
   Poem With Scrutiny ... |103
   Real Classic ... |104
   To the Letters in Your Name ... |106
   A Very Minor Musical ... |107

Acknowledgements ... |109

With simplicity the fantastic animals exit the anguish of their obsession and are hurled from outdoors placed on the walls of rooms where nobody notices them except their creator.

Henri Michaux, *Animal Fantastique*

Your Wing Deck is a Lazy Beetle

your wing deck is a lazy scarab beetle
a lazy beetle
a sonic story
your beetle is lazy
it beelines nothing
your lazy beetle can't beeline
you have a lazy beetle
your beetle is cross-eyed
it's a lazy, cross-eyed, no-good-for-nothing beetle
I hate your beetle
I want a dog and a toad, I want a healthy dog and a healthy toad
I want my toad to ride around on my dog's back
share noodles
I want to learn to sing
I want to learn to sing with emotion and intelligence
my ideas have gone hog-wild
I like expressions I think they act like vices
we have a proclivity towards one another and they make me comfortable
because these expressions are not entirely my own
I am in nature in a leotard
my leotard looks like the jungle
I hang from branches and dominate the sky
sure that's exposure but try it with no hands

Island Scenarios

Split and Raise Force-Field on Deck

In some legendary light I am mistaken
for a blinking field, an analog across the eyes
with a series of horses running forward
like that painting of a wave
where the wave has horses galloping
inside its enormity, and I pity the person
whose vision can't relax to see this moment
sea sweat combing the indistinguishable ardor
the painting I'd always look up to mid-stride
past my boyfriend's bed, he'd say he read an article
about how *surfing was better than sex*
couldn't tell if he agreed or not, I believed
he did but he kept falling back
on how it was interesting and that condescends
the expression like a relaxed sonata, a coming up
for air between being charged with meaning
alas, he said it really was about catching
the perfect wave, and very rarely is someone able
to do this in their life, so the experience transcends
all other actions by its rarity, horses that are the wave
Walter Crane's *Neptune Horses*, no one predicted
I would remember this, I didn't even believe in myself
and hardly realize how inadvertently a perfect wave
sticks with you, a thousand horses galloping
in your mind, a thousand visits to a house
whose deck is sloping down into the unreal, whatever
we do now is like a vision of something coming
undone, a microcosm of *never again*, it isn't sad
the sea salt sticking to the horse's hair
if they are always coming forward in retention
with the wave, are they ever galloping back—
an entire life spent preparing to break, unheard
a lack of any want to amend the past, something
striding, splitting apart and coming back

^ ^

the storm turned
no joke
me a mother prowl
on the dinghy approaching
the service
another kinetic dawn
of lightning and other
blighted objects
filling the bare minimum
of a life-sentence
full of conundrums
out of habit or some habitual swelling
the mother of the lie down and cough drama
a stage coach hangs right to conduct the miscarry
how the shadow becomes a high risen wall
if a prayer is misconduct then
by this I mean
I emanate with all my worth and come forward
and make the epitome June move
with a long wing neck
another junior brainchild
in a tantrum kicking the walls
they crumble like styrofoam
the material becomes category
stuff spreads so thin it's like no wonder
you had a panic attack
and the worthwhile elite steps
down with a tomahawk
the licensed worthwhile A-grade blonde cop
should have been making cheese
last night comes to you
served fresh from absentia who
wouldn't say boo to a goose

Rage Without Meaning

Yesterday I could have sworn I played you
my favorite song, it was about how papa was a rodeo
and mamma was a rock-n-roll band but you didn't feel
the depth of its lyrics in the way I did, as though you
spotted the owl first and never betrayed the emotion
of the experience of what it would feel like to spot an owl
So, again we return to the lonely status of words
if I had said before I played the song that I wanted it to create
a bond, would that have changed things and if so in the universe
or just between my sport and your divorce
I want to erase what you look like all the time, so I can
constantly be detoxified by your beauty and the most ordinary
looking sponge keeps popping up all over the place
just like the acai berry lose-weight-quick scam, I'm not trying
to be impressive, I'm just thirsty and tired and I feel
like I've been on this train all day and that expression *train wreck*
is so dated but I've used it when I couldn't find a better way
to talk about the clutter that'd fill my life, like that one time
at 10am I came home from a boyfriend's house, then went to get coffee
and wound up in a conversation about furniture with a Venezuelan
and I swear I thought he was gay, he was an interior designer
and around the corner we went to his place with his pit bull and I
smoked the stub of an old j and he tried to rape me
I told him many times about how I was unusually strong
for a girl, when my shame level rose I flipped the futon, cursed
the battle and took my chance on a pike-dive into a trash shoot
and hoot hoot that owl would love to resurface in this poem

^^

besides just dreamt you
were there in a closet and I lost my
phone and you had mine and I had
yours and we called each other into
the stubborn night where darkness
was the only thing happening and
you said I'm wholly tired and I told
you to take the kind of drugs that make
you stay awake so you can
travel down the streets to give me
back my phone but you don't care
much for eagles and regalia

Blanket the Storm

small people of the universe
letting one another down
the faint enclosure of your lapping heart
lapping around the pool of your grade b
and c friends, who come over to watch the water
spill onto the deck, be it a non-artery channel
or not, not that there's intentionality
I mean, look at me trying to write
about something sloshing like a lava lamp
the one in the photo behind Dan's desk
but instead all I can think about is his broken-face
there is also blood freely moving
un-homed by skin and dreams and trust
and longing and the spokes still spinning
wandering the streets, looking for some kind
of meaning, a wet dream to wake in, a story
being compromised by the encroaching sadness
in meanings being arbitrary, the lock broken
on the outside of the gymnasium
how we conduct ourselves when we realize
that we've been violated, the little cartoon
clouds following us around, too false
to float in a new direction, we all need
a little recession-proof-umbrella, thin-sky
I tried my entire life not to fuck-up
other people's idea of me, but it still keeps
coming back, mishap in my middle name
I swear there's a theme song for these emotions
but I wouldn't want to see my mouth
scraped like Dan's, thing is, I really wouldn't
mind the part where he did a somersault
over the hood of the car, I kinda miss fleeting
action without a villain or even
unsuspected-momentary-feels-like-death-type-shit

it's hard to be stable, I spend my entire life slightly angry
slightly wanting to obscure my form into lion, at least
I could walk a digitigrade walk, with soft pads nobody hears me
I actually want the neighbors to know that I'm home
so they won't rob me, there's a project I'm almost convinced
I'll never finish, after seeing the colored pencil drawing
of the back of the boy's head, I keep thinking about making
streaming colored pictures on our white walls
I don't live to know small incoherent people of
the universe, rather I want to explore what filling
the white space feels like all the time, that's why
I'm jealous that Bolaño already wrote the book I
was meaning to write, about skywriting with a small
jet engine over the Chilean people, I want to make
people feel so small that they think I'm in the sky

^ ^

to begin the annunciation
about the noun swallowing
the blue whale, let's take
the caps off our pens
and sweat our shorts through
here is something within a
wide terrain that is going postal
evoking digitized nerves, swing
the cut of your memory out
it gets up, walks penguin-style
to the trashcan and is just
a leaflet of your invention
pragmatically speaking
we don't speak within
pragmatics around here
now let the wild geese
of your mind go, begin
by collecting all your
favorite stones, all the
most eclipsed versions
of what you see in a shell
speak from behind that
from within that crashing
and it's inside you
and it's inside you

Is Land

a bridge with a car driving over it
the car driving onto a boat
the boat carries the car across the mainland onto the island
where the little houses live
the little houses you can drive to but only if your car goes
on a ferry across the water
the mainland has more people than the island
home to few who prefer life on the quiet island
as opposed to life on the mainland
the island has water circling on every side
most people don't really care if you are from the island or the mainland
although, it's pretty obvious to a mainlander if you are from the is÷≥land

if you are from the island it is likely that you use less consonants
everything is scaled down
you don't need as many words to draw comparisons
most people are happier than people from the mainland because there
are less people to be competitive with

there are people from the mainland who are really lonely
and don't necessarily have a home
but if you are from the island you have a home or if you don't
there's absolutely no reason why you couldn't sleep on the shore
there are also more ways to eat with less money
there is fruit naturally growing all around
and neighbors are not afraid to invite you over for meals
if you're unable to afford dinner
you are also supposed to show some effort towards working
although, it's also not that big of a deal if you are lazy
laziness isn't condemned but it's also not rewarded
there are few people who are lazy enough to be exiled off the island
if they are exiled, they have to spend
the rest of their lives on the mainland
the mainland sort of has a dictatorship

and the dictatorship is inherently evil
it's evil because that's what people think of
when they think of the word dictator

also, when people go to school
they have to wear denim jackets with corduroys
there is absolutely no differentiation between males and females
partly because they have the same haircut
but also because they are sexless

if you are sexless you don't have to worry about rape

people from the island are not sexless
some people don't understand how this could be possible but it is
because of evolution
it is also due to the exclusivity on the island
and the willpower to develop a taste for sex
thus to pass along sex organs that are valued
valued doesn't mean people have to be manipulated
into sharing your views

values color red
values home
values land
values water

If Land Then Magic

islanders are made of magic
are popular within the subject of inter-polar lifestyles
run into the water and are immediately
the same temperature as the water
leave a tornado of sand granules in their wake

trees behind sway behind blue
islanders fence with bamboo
one more day is all it took
chance is driving egalitarian measures to dominate

time to go get passion
doe a deer a female deer
ray a drop of golden sun
what distracts from attention needs attending to

high on a mountain whittling out who's who
most popular songs are popular on the island for their amusement
if they aren't made to entertain they aren't worth listening to
entertainment is accessible

it takes money to access entertainment
start by caring about the fever in other things
all things are manmade by islanders
islanders are the makers of mankind

make each other human within their own right
if you walk up to an islander you won't get anywhere
you will never get closer
anchors are in effect

the boat has steadied
walk-off and get an ice cream
land on land
the solution to your hair is to comb your hair

what is race for
on the island all is all
no signs of anything different
look around you
the litter is literally glittering

Braved The Sea

I barely feel for a mountain, I come to the sand to embrace infinity
to draw on the back of a vessel: a wood cabin with a red blue jay inside
I saw many men and tried to imagine the world without them
but no one would pay attention, I kept traveling
with or without a sense of time or direction, I felt the way
to my mind was best perceived through imagining
a small child under a microscope
to be seen as a specimen, on a plain glass slide
I swear I tried to teach a man to see indefinitely
but he could not see that he was bigger than the ocean
and the ocean has a bunch of fucking fish swimming around
I put an eye up to his eye, it sure shined the same length
a contrived reference to love, how I caught sail onto a ship
where a celebration for Dred Scott marched on
everyone was trying desperately to wrap a flag around his name
it made me change the way I cared
for weather or rare varieties of plumage
I was mesmerized by the efforts to fight
and caught the intrigue to sail further, I can't claim to have ever
been at arms with the Supreme Court nor struggled with the diversity
of citizenship, I still see a ton of gorgeous boats
and maintain a small installation of an organized court order
I don't see a lot of things coming my way
I use a hook to catch my fish and the severance to pay for it

Whose Land Is Whose

Why is everybody being so particular about whose land is whose?
Universe, what do you have to say for yourself?
<<<provoked theater>><< uncontainable sun>>
less people << shine from behind the rock>>

Yes, that's a large phone you have there.
It's as though you are sitting right next to me.
Well, come to think of it Sadie, if you mix all the letters
up in your name it spells *ideas*; you think
you took that name for no reason. <<cries>>

You take time-travel so sensitively.
We see no water. We see no water.
We can't make what doesn't have water, have water.
<spoon aquarium>

The tunnel is growing bigger not smaller with us behind.
Ragged doll in hand.
A dowel in the other.

Most of what we own has already been
in extinction. Don't put that thread into the river.
The river water meets with the saltwater and we call it brackish water.
If we want to bow-down to it we call it an *estuary*. §^^§

We bow down to it.

On Sand

Finally, we're alive and the only thing that's keeping us
alive is the idea of each other

Finally, we are everything where confusion
gets brushed back to find the purest self

The amends that we've come to are serious
you used to be a runner of a shout

Seaweed washed up, we comb through
to find one another in the surf

It's quiet, then little soft sea things swishing against the sand
you are closest to the water's edge

You having always been closer than me
to everything that matters

Get Your Slip On

next thing to do is to decide how to
react to the next thing
as it passes almost through itself
makes the sentence difficult to abandon
how might a mixture of associations be a good thing?
a dim mountain below what rises up again
it's always the next thing and the next thing
and what comes after can't be true
what awareness a season can bring
as though it's something come undone
still patterned
a naked landscape seeking coverage
a record played
then flipped
played
then flipped again
this isn't boring
this is shape and architecture
the sound of lambs being sheared
saving money for a winter coat
an evening comes again
its shadow carried over
irresistible crack of smile
what's the pleasure drawn in re-ordering?
what's the use of figurative rain?
someone fell down
on top of you
and kept
falling

they called it *gift onyx*
said it came with a map
you could light your turtle on fire
a crapshoot if you will
should have given up
after the broken tooth
hit your lamb
moved through the gate
the field was raw
nothing is open in this city
a city is a field that rings-out light
a taking away of life
in order to give out
something more
hopeful
this is sort of like science
except the controls are in cahoots
with the native species

confused by seasonal habitats
and also dusty eyeglasses for irises
where one is a real eye and one a mouth
a commotion is made to name body parts
and each time graced with presence
more and more intense
the inclusion for gift in motivation
bends the practice into a cone
a cone acts as a funnel
a funnel can allow for small powder
or fluid to move down in an increasingly
narrower gap
it takes a great amount of patience
to subsist off small quantities of food
begin to release your mind
from the control of your stomach
from the wanting and the groaning
without request by the unsatisfied
sustenance gains great importance
in the working of the mind!
topical pursuits become deeper and physical
hopefully once acquired you can see an end
let light funnel through the protracted
arrival from beneath the cellar

III

door wide
wake and able hush
into a lettered stream
a version of the past
strengthens intuition
if lions made shelters
then you'd be bled bored?
ripping the stash from your comprise
each a vessel coming your way
you move on
drift weird adapters
in a hide-away trap
you'd be tucked away and so you are stuck
and resolved in limp disposition
harnessed and lacking sensation
forever stemmed
to some bluer flower
fermentation in unlabeled-emotions
giving into the charged duty of making
turning leaves over in your palm
putting them to rest via illumination
brains for breakfast
targets at the shooting range
k-autodidactic
plexus speaks frizzy
shower under the lamp
and it's just light shattering your face
still breeding down the laurels

adorn the emblem of victory
afterward mad about the devilish arc of boredom
how it comes to sprout
then downside exceeds into
excess drifts of snow matching the weather maps'
exceedingly-anticipated-locations

not that stability isn't a good thing
and hasn't given rise to insight
like how I can look and speak and just plain feel
tethered to some noble-domestic-situation
an apt limb dangling to decide if I *still* love you like *that*
of course
                    I do

no need to justify this indented margin
it is only for effect
solitary and manageable
please don't come begging
if a backbend is all I can do

first stepping in-and-out of the rain
Eric gathers a goose
he just bends down and picks it up
says, *it's for me lady*
he rations his crush
this is a novice kind of night
broodier and biennia
she'll come over
stands in front of the gap in the door
a wild public stance
shotguns a glass of fine ale
this is like a stupid puzzle
where one piece is bent
and nobody has a place
in your heart

I am still and still and should be
someone else's problem
my parents raised me like
    this
dormitory of three enigmas
how might this represent a
Turkish gimlet?
conceptual crawdads?
achieve winnowing classifications
searching for some other way to
pronounce ourselves
not man and wife
but she-horse
and universe

it is a curse!
split my mind so hard
over the blimey
Watergate
this is the news
a station agent
sits at home and sketches out pilots
for America's greatest conversations
over natural resources
my real life is like saltines and cheese!
hooray I just made somebody's day
the villains of course
divorce your ghost-boyfriend
in a wardrobe closet
channel
an uncle who's mathematically
the opposite of Rod Stewart
like looking in the mirror
then turning your head really fast
and looking back again
double-take as an infraction on you
and who you want to be

Triggermoon Triggermoon was the title
of my friend's first book
she wrote like half an animal and half a person
she depicts vague orientations between woman and child
amends a map between various universes
between intention and free association
between image and information
a wild kind of night
she is still here
and there

slip into a dialog about infrastructure
at a time when I know little about building
building met the sky through a glass dome
an old reptile at a billiards table
crawls around the dowels
while another is seated at a fiery booth
there is an old saying
what comes in
must go out
believe it today more than ever
a furnace burning my bank account
feel like jumping into a pool of jelly!?
slander and vixen
as if a massive boa constrictor
could cry
it's so pretty
the skin so shiny
these sentences are all connected
though lacking a continuity that is recognizable
to the overly-cognitive eye

get your slip on
maybe for purpose
maybe for delegation
tonight is my time to swim softly
out at sea
like inside someone's camera lens
you see yourself swimming
while the action is archived
you are sheltered from the sun
with one of those wide-brimmed papyrus umbrellas
it is a mellow image
like a sterling-silver formation of boats
I gave you the party I was meaning to throw myself
a house full of roses
a bath of celebrity photos
for once there's no impulse to censor
I have an epistemological relationship with a certain kind of kismet
flare guns at my ice sculptures
belly-dancers at my funeral
everything is Freddie Mac ruined this country
that is a go zone
this is not
it is the reality of the scenario

filter into the room quietly
with sustained laughter
showered and then wrecked
the black ball in the middle of the square
the white filling in like sound
an apocalypse of the now
modern man is so unkind
dry with a bone to gnaw on
some aftermath
or birth defect
covered in scars
laid down the way
showed what's terminable
slipped indeed

without indifference the smallest space
is entered in absolute certainty
you lay your arm across the way
as in *presentation*
I present to you *this day*
and *that way*
we negotiate still about very little
as in met with the proper council
as in represented our view-points
stood upon the open wooden deck
and discussed what relevant scenarios
we could think of
it is often not enough
to keep the day going
to keep the cargo from slipping
we try to line up our shoes
to show the weather
to glimpse the back-bone of the law
but with nothing and nothing
and still staying put
the smallest things remain intact

the artifice in desire to remain hidden
doesn't get you anywhere
not for the neglected
and dolphins swim towards their names
maybe there is a reason
our clothes are ready-wear
grab them when you hit-up an obstacle course
there is a time when you are not my most loyal friend
but then again
it does not come often
I have introduced an episode in the
Life According to a Part-Time Chef
its color is something that lies down and cries
and craps a lot
a lesson like a pilgrim's death
where nobody wanders serenely
look around
there's a chapter in your life that you're not privy to
writing without interference
prying into an occasional haze
something useful comes of decay
maybe wearing a suit is a useful weapon
you stand in for a big ram
it's the Chinese New Year
underachievement is this year's goal

darts and the word for *lake*
filling in the slip with mud
the catch with dice
the fall with slander
if it was a tribal day
you'd look perfect
you're perfection
a yoyo wound down
you sit fastened in boudoir flair
it's enough to set a woman on fire
it's enough to be the first
to talk
to tattoo about the dream
bleeding sideways
like fresh kill
like someone's watching you
one shoulder behind the next
WILD TURKEY DAY

three glass-tones
fitting in a cauldron
one beak pecking outside
twins are in the trees
baby birds
mouthful-o-worms
here you look out
then recover
look back in
then realize
grass floats in a bath
you bomb
but so what

invisible ballet played out in your chest
fit for it
for romantic tropical light and ease
for a republic of station wagons
and singing sisters
you fell down to the music
pulled out a party streamer
used the coral to quote-end-quote mark your rhythm
will dance for scallops and cherries
visit the restaurant
you've been meaning to chaperone your kids on dates to
they are there
without you
giving you the middle finger
an encamped kind of night
pluck anything you don't see fit
it's beginning to blind through
raspberry cake
fuck you earthquake
last night rocked
jungle gym of fever
clandestine enterprise for the young up-and-comers
it's okay to achieve greatness
with all those lost orgies
baked-young skin cancer
a twister in your thighs
17 and still stuck on the high beam
can there be a day to celebrate failure?

SMOTHERED IN EMU MILK

EVERYONE THAT IS OUT THERE LOOKS REALLY COLD

I feel stuck in a viscous of old laundry, trash, billboards and an un-recreational landscape. I crowd the floor with my disco nature. A crouch dance and subliminal stargazing douchiness. I wipe my hands of all the mess already made. Eventually, some kitchen will come through. Have a swell time setting your foot off this planet, like you can hyper-extend an appendage into a moonscape. Some silly old person told me that they would do anything to visit a planet other than earth, but I advised them sweetly, *shush nobody wants to hear about your dreams*. They bore other people and especially me. Check out the women in their nature masks at home phoning in clerical ditties and tax-breaks. I break into all fours and scat across the floor, doe-like, tracking some reformed species. I reckon it's about time a figure tore through the gate, a bio-kingdom for other animals to grange.

I CAN'T STAND BEHIND YOU

When Justin wanted to title his book *Safe Word*, I told him I thought it was too specific of a gesture in one particular direction, or something like that. By the way I was just in the hall thinking what would my safe word be, and I came up with *masculine shower*, which doesn't make sense, which is why I'm sharing. I usually think a poem begins somewhere within unreasonable depths, and then when you type-it-up, you assume responsibility. Yesterday I hurt where you bowl, before I even left the house for bowling! Now it's an infectious tear in my skin between thumb and forefinger. My pinky broke three times and now permanently sticks a little further out. I will not show you a YouTube video of the operation that would straighten my joint. How some organizing principal behind poetic order drives us to receive utter contentment. I have learned content manager programs for uploading new media to websites but I still won't put you in my poem. Well, I wish I had deleted the prom-dress scene, as you love skin more. This is a recoded nexus for stupidity. Plug all your formatted emotions into my system and I'll spit out emoticons. Motorboat between your buoyant breasts. Time floats up while I swell down. I can't stand being behind you. Most subjects contain a multitude of errors, like where did the car go when it died, it died with no dudes in it, just froze to the sidewalk and never moved. Lonely fuck. This is a blessing but you just don't know it yet.

THE CORONATION

He calls that nail *shiny*, the afterglow of hammer in hand. And the people across the street with their Christmas tree still lit— it's March 11th and I'm sitting at the kitchen table, pizza crust in hand and one ripe-thought casting a translucent haze over the oven. There is nothing to laugh about and I'm all done making science. You win the award and I'll make a ceremony for you. Crown the top of your head with a Judas Priest song.

SUMMER IS X

Summer is a firefly in a jar with melting butter. A kind of almost math, the arbitrary variables to complete an equation. Summer is X. Likely to combust without water. The play without words must have been a good story. The story about the window being just closed enough. Summer inside a monsoon is a continuous cooling off. A clover doesn't know shit about luck. Words beat against the jar, wings, almost to blame.

LIVE HOOKING FOR THIS TUMBLR

It's okay. One of these days you'll see the genius in my work and wish that you had accepted all my poems. But this isn't a utopia, it's a train, and it fucking stinks, and idylls and I forgot my cliff bar in my other purse— and I'm feeling adverse and formally ignorant. I'm bored and not bird-like in appetite. For I have killed a whole lot of something. It's okay. I hate your poems too. It's okay. I give-up, we cannot all be perfect talents. Have you seen that episode of 30 Rock where Jenna just shits on those kids? I bet that feels good, like this poem. I'm going to go buy tear gas tomorrow, that way next time I'm in the Tenderloin alone, I won't have to run, I can just spray. I'll have to be sexually harassed first, but that's easy, I'll just wear some tight ass skirt and whistle some little tune. Bring attention to myself then propel a culprit into many levels of shame. *You asked for it*, I'll say and then pull a snuggy from my bag, so that by the time there's some live action on the scene I'll be looking like a potato sack. Who's gonna want to interact with that? *Call it what you will*— my mind is worth a million suckled titties... How's that for the cat's meow?

HOLD HANDS WITH SOME SOFT SOBER FEELING

Hold hands with some soft sober feeling with a lamb. Ee i ee i oh, but I won't let go. I promise I'll stay sober the rest of the night. I won't lean over in my sleep and yell strange things, angry, like an atom-celled creature. I apologize for all the times I've run into the walls and shouted, ordinary silence has an opacity I can kneel down to, but not be made carbon-copy of. Make neat stacks of papers and chaperone kids to school plays, ballets and symphonies. I've held hands with many strangers stranger than myself. My brother says I'm the weirdest person he knows, that is blood for you. I just want to plant burial circuses in critique for some fraudulent ritual, be made mayor of an ant farm. I stepped on a red anthill once and cried childlike, freaked out for weeks that the animals got inside of me. Are ants animals *and vice-versa—* I love saying that to everything, like a shattered throughway.

AIN'T GOT NO WINGS

For sure I can fly but I'm done doing it. Ain't got no wings like an owls, or night vision capabilities to deliberately see through the black. Our eyes just don't work like that. I've got mad skills though, I'm just using them gingerly these days—there's a hook but you'll have to find it yourself—I'm too busy writing this thing— to actually act it out. I pretend to be a guide at the New Museum, locating the conceit behind each work, sharing particular concepts and theories for art-making intentions, to induce the audience into intensive listening, and to help them see what might not be clear to an out-of-practice eye. I purposely leave my notes on my desk, to flirt with the idea that someone will steal from them. I'll end up the chair of this-or-that department. Take home molds of milk bottles and baby snap peas. For art does not tell but it reveals. Tinkering away at an installation before god gives up on us all.

NOW THAT EVERYTHING HAS DISSOLVED

Now that everything has dissolved in sweet camphor your inner animal awakes from the sedation of a long winter past. You jungle up in your bones and stretch your torso like a fresh piece of canvas. A floury corporal pushes aside its dream and seeks invasion. Burgeoning beneath the wreckage you glimpse the possibility of ever-extending happiness, like a cartwheel with perpetual motion churning you up on your side and in various directions. Equal to the luminosity that you felt after reading a book about inhabiting space and custom designing a house with fur walls and endless aquariums. Under the underpass to the osteria you find the hostess, where roosters wade on the influx of lilacs. How many prescriptions did you take to survive this winter? Why keel over to our surrounding native species? How the foxlight gloats with such dim reason. How adapting to the environment is the same thing as yielding to the conclusion of an everyday brush with fate. Like the joke where the man walks into a bar and tries to order emu milk...

CHOKED-UP LEADERSHIP

I put this position of leadership into the hands of children who aren't afraid to fly. I take this position of a choked-up leadership role, with no way out of it. I put the reins on and am dragged by wolves. Dragged through the snow and across the frozen pond to the area surrounding the cabin that is also near the woods, by the way, I call *that* a schoolhouse. Although, to speak referentially about something that doesn't exist is to refer to an episode in the mind's eye that takes on a winnowing shape, or the translucency of what I no longer know. I have tried to snow, to make myself snow. It's a dark-hole in there, you see, I'm offered no lamplight and the residual effect after a certain period of time is one of circadian entrainment.

NOW THAT THE HANDSHAKE IS A FAILED GREETING

Now that the handshake is a failed greeting, we press our mouths together and leave a wet slick sway of betrayal all the way down. We sting because we got a bucket of jellyfish thrown onto us. We all just like totally die. Everyone is hanging out in "heaven" looking ridiculous, eating chocolate éclairs and talking about the barely minted universal saying, "if you slay at socialism, you will forever be loved." Up here love isn't that big of a deal, so cashing in on this notion involves a super small exchange rate. Anyhow you don't acknowledge time and time doesn't acknowledge you. After jumping around on a few clouds you get bored and start to paint with glitter. Nothing is metaphorical anymore.

BURGEONING BENEATH THE WRECKAGE

Who is the author of beating cancer— in need of a serious lifestyle-change? An event is coming near you that will absolutely ruin your life. Get hip to it before the wave hits, its crash is fatal. If the accident lacks exposure the media will turn around and penetrate the fuck out of you. Are you listening? All I'm asking for is a little forgiveness. A little kindred-soul. Don't get me started talking about these trees: maple, deciduous, eucalyptus, pine, palm, plum, willow hanging out in your backyard. Not lacking any exposure. Showing it all like Scarface. Guide us all down to death. This is the best season for a dreamteam.

CALLING FOR RENDER

I feel complete, though this status is pending, to be decided once the hybrid between grass and flow fractures into anew species. The one counted on, for my demands to be met, given any circumstance of brooding and being host to all feelings and no real grasp on reality. To be the one challenged by thought. Obnoxious by the cinematic critique of others' language. I can't just expose myself. Why open that kind of drama. That rebuttal with livid proof. The fleshed piston arrives; the flower reveals itself to the world, as does the world.

FIELD DORSAL

I am the crowd and in it wet with ridicule of dayglow. Here a fence is needed but water won't will it. Into primordial beam I long to be an echo chamber but keep ruining my chances. Pleasure is only felt if it is well received. And maybe redressed. Red dresses filled with crawl. I can put a room in here. A closet. A chaperone. And still you won't find a sexual scenario that doesn't fault in encumbered play date espionage. Any excuse to unwind the season. Any age to become. It is miles to the nearest unknown place. It all seems so easy.

STRIP CLUB FOR VARIED ARTIFACT

You're the first of the last before everything else was silent. Before centers. Before inevitable growth in ions. Things that look open could still be closed. Same with a hand in the pocket, how it might still wear a glove. Inhospitable attention brings a series of la la las. Haters in the playfield.

UNCOVER THE REALM

Think like today was your last. Raise your hands those of you who have absolutely no hang-ups. No glitch or punk ass boss to deal with. Healing from the fraud of la di da like it looks cool not to give a fuck. Not to represent. Not likely an intimate response to the cavernous future. Of stealth and dark waves. There are rooms for mistakes, that shit is human, and land, and plant. Like a quilt of gold floating down the river.

FOUND EXPERIENCE

Seems phenomenal that we can just go out into the world and have these experiences. That we don't have to be anybody but ourselves. But then again we build empires of thought and majestic scopes of billowing intentions, more so then could be imagined. Lit the thing you couldn't think of on your own into a ferocious fire, in a good way, the way setting one thing down implies that you're sure to pick up another. Fork and pitch are wondrous freely things, nature claiming its sway. Bent till the hill ungirths the train, vault of my own human ears and stereoscopically flea, neigh past the artichoke plant. Plant whatever feet you can find on the ground. To be filled with many mouths of rainwater, the drought seizes to exist. Mix a mermaid with an octopus with a bottle of tequila and the whole body-thing will float overall sea.

MELATONIN

My bus does well with your roads. Almost like a watery thing. Slipping where slippage is implied. It attends to your road, curves with your curves, breaks when you want it to. You're gonna have to be real patient with me, it can take a little time to get there. A little gas and oil. I don't mean to overuse the natural resources; I mean I too wish I rode by horse, bareback along the Chilean mountains. A quest towards over sized independence, blazing stars and saddleback lunches. Broad terrain, how we curve when you curve and still gleam hope from ridiculous dreams.

WITHOUT INHERITANCE

Wow, you abbreviate your archipelagos, like looking a seahorse in the eye and boo-hooing, telling it you don't believe in it. I wave my hand at a party passing by. Might as well throw in the towel on this whole "not drinking thing." Tin tin and rattle rattle. Flick one of those tiny smart cars off the sidewalk. Wingdings and mustard does easy with camouflaging the scent of my dream. I may forgo all this pride and get up and go make myself a milkshake. The fake sword has fake blood on it, but the sheath is real and filled with eggplant and pauper demons. This is a way of catering to a large crowd. It's not a private story. The air is not winsome. Dust and burn and ash and move.

REPURPOSED WONDERBREAD

It's a cluster fuck of a day. A cistern chapel bombed out. A rugby match looking like carpentry. A real cheese sandwich. Institutions within reach. Live amoeba. Retracted throat muscle. Biblical miscellany and figments litter the city. Washed up hope. Philosophical machinery. Empty forty. A ground inspector on LSD. Make rational not love. Volcanic Island. Sauce on the sly. Say it again and I'll bruise you more.

RESCUE COMPASS

We are trying to comb through our minds to figure out exactly what we want to say and how. Slope of skill and wild fleeing the mind into a somersault of *yes, you can have my baby*. I spot rescue, was relieved by slender routine. Still a search can also degrade, when you are looking for something truly real. Movies fuck us up. Think, replicating what you see, levitation into false embers and wooden ledges. Where so can tone be sewn into intrepid language, a lustful appliqué? We turned sound with our minds and oh ledges how they grew. We trouble a frame. Torqued more stars, till dusk do us part.

DID A LITTLE TURN

Hole punch the card and get a free latté next time. Exposure is identity and vis á vis. A visionary pets a manchild's hand and tells him true love is the only way he'll get his shit together. Adult pressure flees in the shape of eagles leaving a mountain peak. Eclipsed sun scaled back draws the onset indicative of a panic attack. To skirt around the legitimate sacrifice. If negation need to be met then he must listen to the vision. If not to visit his own grave hundreds of years from now. If not to be made new in natural shaped things. To not outsource the panic and die with no expression. Wilts and dioramas of achievement in the shape of native wit and he has manganese. He frees all domestic pets and the prairies are littered with cats and dogs and it still takes two to tow the rosebuds around town.

RUINED AND RUINOUS

Pull vegetables from the ground. Asunder. Asunder. Unusual usage of tone. Tonal inequity. What hot hot sun you have there in the South. Never have been so soundless. Sound is something escaping. The cruelty of the sky hitting another sky, then making large Atlanta drops, like wind is the escape goat. Been meaning to harvest something. Been meaning to ripen. That window looks like a cloud or vice-versa. These walls are so hidden and strung out; not saying anything. Tis' ruined, and ruinous when people say things like "if these walls could talk," well if these walls here crumbled you'd get struck across the cheek for such dialog. Like you all talk and talk, then there is a motion made and you move towards it. Like the ocean lives in that one guy's baseball cap and you keep restoring your vision to focus harder on his boat. His billy-club. It's a terrible offense to be struck so hard. To be so off putting. What an usual way to speak these things. What a hard light to turn on.

Starts in Herds

I felt rich and so tested fine
leathers for quite sometime
wore thick armed bracelets
with eagle paired earrings and sang
phonetic-intercourse-themed-songs
beneath the Topaz Valley
was wrestled down by a carpenter
bought him cocaine and tote bags full
of champagne
lifted him across a lagoon
where a trusty steer yielded to him
door-step upon door-step selling shampoo
and foot cream
a hypnotherapist came one day to ruin him
is what she did
but she actually wanted
to convince him of his loyalties
not by ogling the curvature in his spine
no no but by putting him to rest
communicating by shellacking his inner-core
she wanted to condition the opalescence
in his mind to feel more
to be a man of modern riches
not that foot cream wasn't a passion
of his but he should be signing large
installments of artwork in worldwide museums

❖

and beyond thought and idea,
there's a young silo of sound
it's not an obtrusion
rather a Ritalin inflicted can-can light
neither with or without opacity
or an instar landing on your shoulder
young ideas, you are young thoughts
there are bills to pay and fire-escapes
to climb without reason into the
brass night, whatever, when you ring
my neck with anger it's also just
the weather being cancelled from
continuing, I know as much as you
know that there's no void to turn against
and with free will, it will keep turning

thoroughly confused by this mission
of overwrought joy
I am now pouting in my bathing suit
sorting through bins of scuba gear
I went to wash down while staying awake
closed the door to the water closet
put my body all the way under
felt the itch of finger glue and
the putty in passing around wine
passed out passed in-and-out of
various sounds from the street
some sounding like a deer claw
walking across cement
how the road
is what we need in order to visit friends
but not them
bended leaf upon bended tree
can the mountain tell us that we are lost
that we've composed everything without compassion
that we should quit our jobs
write haikus about the value of
fatigues and emotions trailed like a slug
I want to be a prison
break-free-tour-guide
show those rusted-heads a bird sanctuary
for once I'd like to lay down blue pillows
for someone other than my own name

closed every door entered but still
felt an inconsolable sense of grief
put up with the thousand YouTube
videos of my large ass
though this fostered
an inkling of defenestration
was reminded that I was loved
remained love
art town of bobbing police
an end came as a beginning to something
all the shouting that went on and thus
continued closing doors
the collection of rookie cards
flapjacks and saw-tooth puzzle pieces
how these each became an element
worth building on if not even glued together
handsome grand stands of patio furniture
how my ankles rubbed against its plastic
I became a pool to jump into
at the very beginning
of killing time I began you
you began me and poison
became the law
the law a centripetal force
pulling us in and pushing us
back outside the equator
where no stars

the experienced stranger
arrives with leashed intuition
and prefabricated rainbows,
a bevy of salt and water in
a glass dome like a framing
of Jupiter in a half-way house
you walk in on a man eating
a sandwich, he takes on
the most meaningful characteristics
about a man, one who likes
to eat and lurk with a nascent
expression of desire, this
is a form of blindness, this is
a perfectly stable way of not
writing, this is a way of using
the ingredients inside a sandwich
as a kind of code operandi, what
historical pepper, what lipid
lettuce, what's a lip to a cow—
the equivalent of hiring a motivational
speaker to help you talk to a stranger

care about nothing
then care about everything
and fall full of trust
into the arms of all my fans
putting the rain together
how hammered the blue sky
looks drunk on its own color
the hip side still just another
way to pronounce low tide
it barely touched the joint
just about tugged the lace
and pulled the room down

I am a gateway drug
my problem is that I
get inside you and infect
you, I am infectious
my vocabulary is a curse
and my window, a harpoon
of light, I make your insides
rattle like tight rope-tension,
a tenor drum, I also drum
monkey-style in your head, that
beat for social dominance,
this art is not for sale
I've actually raised the stakes
for moving day, I'm selling all
my goods at twice the price
I paid, why, because I can and
I want to get laid and move to
Japan, there is no restaurant below
my apartment now, and I'd love
to dine on the dining room floor, what
a spectacular way to live far
from the pragmatic gluttony of
piracy, the web is really sucking
it all out of us people, there's a
horse cry

care about nothing then
care about everything
and drive through a wax
museum on a scooter
with Bill Clinton
cheers lapsed in waves
of bravado and fictitious
yore spike the tea
then relax on the red carpet
and try to bite the nose
off one of those more
perfected sculptures
gets about hundred °s in here
and they start to melt
whole room of wax
and a scooter stuck in stall
and Bill Clinton
Bill Clinton and

care about
nothing
then care
about everything
spread love juice
make noise in the apartment
pull every book off the shelf
and act like they're hot coals
you walk across to achieve braveness
put whatever light you can hold in
your hand and blow it through
a kiss to everybody missing
the world sustains itself for a moment
pity flags are waved
you march on through the snow
and lo and behold the whole world
is a living room lapping-up buttermilk
now hold your eyes all the way open
and see what a scene becomes
called the stupid apocalypse
no way it's not an attempt out
of unspecified beliefs
not that there is laundry to be done
again the fridge
is missing every color

I came up with a new song
about fashion last night
I kinda screamed it

FIFTEEN WHALES UNDER
MY BLACK NAILS

Entropy Poems

Entropy: Take the Stinger Out

obliterate the tall tall grass
freak-show side-curve it
ever heard of it
considering a possible make-
over total invisible marketable
future-me yet undesignated
un-designed
could redesign it
redesign me then market it
to see if people like it
it being new me
me yet to be formed
stood tall on the sandy beach
all the trees that I could climb
were for safety if I lost
the proton of vast-perspective
my high-tops will be suede-elope-star
converse banded to my neck
the pentimento scarf
I bought for fifty cents
at an Italian hopscotch
see winter being tossed
through a lantern
five bones for the
hero who saved my
soul just saw cliffhanger
a documentary different from bats
little clutches to the wall
except maybe the
sound of what potential
will be bounced back
outside from the truth
the moss is starting
to
atlas

Entropy: Instead of the Crux

sneeze attack
on the Jesus Christ
statue out back
I'm a hood monger
burnt *the edges*
off a map [to halo]
the rim
that's what she said
she also had no problem
demonstrating so much
more than I could
ice that you'd like
to put in the fire
there is when
we claim told you so
if we could be
received more often
and certainly I am
not enough poet
and certainly I am
not enough ghost
even within the half
way marks I still
don't even come
close to recognizing
my own god
the face of a zebra
launches at me and I
feel the tempo
of an Icelandic song
coming into existence
and then stifling into
my flaws are the
great uncles of all
my pasts

Entropy: Defined by the Loss that I have to Reconsider

stark lit the bomb off my chest
slit the throat off my guilt
built me a small unicycle
that only one person could ride
and only one person could build
Fryer's law of science
choice of day
clean slate gray
not even a pillbox could
fit all my thrills
The Keiser Tied Tie
for evening dress
is to be worn with standing
wing soft or semi soft fold collars
already tied by experts for
the man in a hurry
it's Regiment U.S. Patent Officer
is from New York
it's just a regular guy
who talks a lot
I really wanted
to give him head on that raft
kept telling him it would be
even more like floating
I can see potential beyond
an ordinary person
who doesn't feel joke or *syncope*
or knows how to express laughter
crawl out from behind my face
and feel so much more than other people
a noble starling takes flight
and I smash the instinct of
another gone
survivor

To Talk Its Way Out of Me

«

First make a history of hair
whatever is inside, we make light
of, we have no words, words that are terse at least
(Beer gut, Bill Knott, Beirut) at least the
lesson we've tried to teach each other
is one of shame (that's what I keep
showing myself) we ride around
the argument, hint towards a misreading
but you allude to the Corsicans
with such poor grammar, his trade,
his flag, his bandana, I have
no name

««

people want to circumvent the obvious
pretend it doesn't exist, (cowards
of the dark frothing sea) I point everything
out as if the ritual-of-flaw were something
to surrender to, we put ourselves in
dumb positions then pity ourselves
when we break, you want to say
whilst we surge through
the night, instead, take for example
cardboard, how we could build
a home with it
the frontlines gathering touchwood

»»»

nighttime moves out of color (out of context)
I know that I am doing this thing
using the language that came before to inform
the choices I make next, the problem isn't that
I'm doing this now, in these poems, it's that I'm
doing this in all arenas of life, flexing and
pointing to my guns then thinking about pulling
a trigger, it's tricky, I don't want actions
to fall hot-molten then solidify hematite and
turn arrowhead, this leaves no room for the un-
predictable to spawn fins, become unwieldy
creatures that cast no shadows, wrecked
unto ourselves, forever stuck inside this poem

»»»»

smoke signals, smoke signals
go throw yourself
a little puck to battle, night is growing into a solid
barrier that needs to be charged through, my friend
made a video through a series of steps like William Kentridge
she recorded herself running full speed several times
into a wall, then recreated these images with pencil
and charcoal drawings over-and-over again
then photographed each image and ran the still shots
together in a thread to make the video of running
into the wall, something we all should
do a little more often

《《《《《

make something come again by thinking
the slit of an eclipse allows you to take
a little piece of it with you
the fattest person on stilts, a building
ballooning out where the upper half can't
be supported by the lower half, the memory
of darkness when the darkness consumed
you, you leave a car crash behind, don't
turn your back on a wave, a fire, yes
turn away, you left and never came back
and by this I mean *didn't give up*

《《《《《《

when the rain falls in sheaths across
the window, all the papers from your manuscript
don't add up to this, and they're stacked
just about everywhere, I keep telling you that
one day you'll make it up to me by writing
about my life and that for now I forgive you, even
after witnessing the single snail that survived
the sidewalk, something beside itself in an
understatement, tonight, wikipedia the
meaning of *dashboard*, let me know if silver
tooth is acknowledged because I know you
got that cap after slamming into those bull horns
on the front of your brother's truck
data can't be consistent all the time
what are you looking for: moxie, hubcap,
the spiraling of time dying inside of us
with all this rain, and all these wheels
and the illusion we understand relativity
this one time is sure to be more desperate than
any other, you still can't talk it out of me

»»»»»»

even if staying meant there'd be no leaving
leaving made it completely impossible to stay
checking into the hostel to hang between a non-existing space
resting on a stain, a leaving
of somebody else, there is no patience coming slowly out
of my body, on the down-side, prediction sucks
it's not a toy-with-your-mind-kind-of-game
I'd like to fast-forward the part where I'm a civil servant
to the *The Killer Whale and the Artichoke* cartoon
as if the artichoke is going to raise its spiky leaves like a morning star
(also known as a holy-water sprinkler)
this medieval club-like weapon, (also
known as a goedendag)
makes contact with the whale, waged war
made old school
I love antiquity, enough to die
by its grace

»»»»»»»»

we are staring at the longest walkway we might ever take
you pull a tooth from the animal
that's robbed your identity like you're at a freedom festival
as if we are members of the skyline, saluting our obituaries
as if I'm inside the body of a white dying albino shark
it's like looking at the sun for too long, what is it about hatred anyway—
why does it eventually kill us— the willingness for confrontation
to be the arrival at intimacy, not all touch-and-go is how it should be
this walkway will end at the dogwoods, we'll lay petal upon
petal upon petal, until we can't feel evil anymore
as if time could be talked out of the small of my back
as if heat were ever really a wave

{»«}

thanks for coming over to my poem
I admit to my overuse of I, and also for the direct liability
that in relationship to the current text some of this information
may or may not be accurate, and that I am at the center
I admit that I am beside myself and the reckless exterior of continuing
this presupposes your interest, there are several gaps in time,
which I'm not able to make up for, so you might have to fill
those in yourself be a language chief, forget all about me, I'm just here
to guide you, I really want to make you feel better about your life
I'm thinking if I talk to you in this way that you might open up to me
there is so much more to be said, and how deeply troubled we all are

Dear Ultimatum,
Here is what I think should matter;
the foggiest memories, those repressed are lighthouse-valuable
it is another kind of simple error to be American, there is the bowl
that you have taken across the road with you, you have carried it
to the place that matters, drop things into its center, let it spiral down
like a drain, count the conditions that brought you here, to this
stability, standing so willfully proud, yet a little light on the humor
you can't take yourself so seriously, after hours of beating the dead
horse to a pulp, the blinds softly pulled down around you
you can't take light anywhere, there is this letter also, that I'm meaning
to write to you, I've been meaning to mean addresses, to mean that
there is a distinction, I've been meaning to call upon hospitality
please snip a piece of your hair for me, place it under your pillow
then leave, I can't stand being pinned by your sunlight, there are
other rooms, and within those rooms there are even smaller rooms
and within those rooms there are closets, and within those closets
there are dressers, and within those dressers there are cigar boxes
and within those boxes there are pillboxes and within that pillbox
there is a pill, now take that pill, swallow it well, well down
that throat, now leave all those entrances as exits, and go exist
elsewhere, there is so much space just waiting to be filled with you
Love, it's entirely up to here

A Theory of Feathers and
Warrior Gear

Not For June

it's not for june
it's not for spit
or aerodynamic youth
you bloody shield
you friendly hypocrite
I shot this mouth's pirate video
it is insane
unlike the posse I possess
under my under garment
under my robe of warm and fright
you frigid month you Monday holy monster
are we scared of each other or are we earth day's competitor
it is such a foul day a mouth of clay it is wet in this hammock
there is bridge and bone to fight for
we defend we develop weapons
we fight parade mans
it's like a hunger game but you are A-List classified artist
I love you
I surrender to you
I will knit the rest of the world for you
be my bridge
be my bride
be my sweet angel
it is tempting when I'm caressing you
and lying down in the bath with you
it is not a hideous thing
it is the best time
I'm so excited let's be again
you start here
I'll do the rest

Intergalactic Battles

the thing is I think really I want nothing
and honesty isn't always a good thing
people don't have patience for boldness
say you are willing to walk up and say anything
I am saying and so knowing
I am bad ass
you meet someone and say
let's have laborious sex
and shy away and go away and never come back
it is the equinox so I am acting funny
I love to be in love and then I don't
not because it is snowing today but because I forget how
and so quickly learn again
and in that moment achieve utter and complete in loveness
you feel like home, I tell you and mean it
lean past your roots, encompass the carnage of guilt
you are a human factory of forgiveness
you have let everything go and you still keep it all
as if holding a thing was a real spaceship
hooray we are eager but both broke and unfit
if ever there was an oval we'd be at its center
demystified purpose of invention
so propose to me, I say, *so rid the guilt*
except, it is infectious and commoditized
we have a fever with the chills
are lost between two time-zones

The fifties are over
I need a chariot pick-me-up

The Yellow Crocus of Down Under

Sifted through the late crowd
wasn't going anywhere in particular.
Felt the find. Blah
wire and deep commotion. Felt I was
an extraneous person to my actions,
being less involved meant
I didn't have to be impressionistic, pulled
down the curtain of a very minor musical. Started to compose
false drama, a stone throw away from
ingenuity. I have begun to think about
what it would be like to spend my entire
life on the edge of sanity. The frequency of those
illusory visits are such that
they ignite sub-par feline crawl. I constantly don't care or if
I do, I don't have a baby to lose. And the big balloon
keeps trafficking through my window, I'm fat
between its red and green zones. There's no need to recognize
yellow. Eat. Sleep. Caucasian.

Poem With Scrutiny

I am obtrusive when alone
not only thinking of myself
with many questions
you are made entirely from assumptions
create panic in your main-dome
it's a hemispheric thing
I apologize for being so considerate
at night the lab-man calls with the results
I have a tiny tumor but it's only a ladder in mind
a day later it's reached the size of a pigeon's egg
I bludgeon all my problems and takeoff
wade into an Olympic sized pool
you are jealous of my notoriety
to be pinned-down by strangers
the pool has become thimble-sized
the water had to be drained, they kept saying
I was eager for the voices
to go away but not the medicine
in redundant time we lapse our mainstream
self-propulsion right up to the brink
making brave animals shy
making quarters spin on the bottom
if you shout it is because I am waiting
for you to love me
the way I want to be loved
night is generous with its blackness
and nobody to blame

Real Classic

shit gone array
back to the dominant
obvious truthful
power struggle
worn warm
into the night
fuck-up punches
classical arts
a sexual manner of speaking
then the majority confidently going to sleep
all plan and no action
nothing innovative nor romantic to speak about
the lumberyard full of trees is so obvious
thou hath nothing to speak of
as being holier than thou
egg-planetarium
equivocal natures to say the least
subjunctive measures need to be taken accordingly
according to physics and the ratios of quantum mechanics
don't you wish that someone cared about your responsibilities
the depths of the sea at this late hour with all these silent bells
the interrogation of truth is all around us
we happen to be witness to a cause
with all these empty hands
trying to grope at other people's sides and nipples
the path departure in a setting sunset
into a sense of crunching ribs
ad hoc available at a minimum
and the camper man closing the tent flap
loose light sputtering in as time waves
when they really are light waves
oh how daylight savings raptures with our kiss
perturbed or not this midnight hour offers such a stint the classics
and for that matter you hate the classics
rather chute of social wealth

dip in and dip out
feeling in a hot tub has never felt lighter
the body weighs nothing
when you recollect that you are in it
could easily kill time with all this figure work

To the Letters in Your Name

I want to wreck you
in the dark
am eager to show you my parts
where the play works and memory
shoots through
each scene like
a transfer of energy
a willingness to unleash
fissure nets
a bit of stereotypical gloating
light around the room
consumed by testimony
summer carries me
leave the wine alone
ditch town
take out a huge loan
color in all the windows
black and hideaway
like I've never wanted you
farm the gully and wait
and wait and wait
find me buried
several jars with antiquated verbs
under orange trees
careful not to respond
responsibility
I haven't envisioned to occupy
what theater
what overhang
what an ugly way to justify a cause
remove black from the windows
to be reconsidered
evening breaks
my only motivation

A Very Minor Musical

warned incontrollable men
about their want for lion manes and
tropical fish, this desire implodes
and bursts earth back in their money-face
be more careful with what you wish
to fuck, desire is innocuous, however
truth creates barriers between you and
the larger sense of world, historical facts
run the gamut these days, more puppet than
librarian, doesn't everyone wish they
had a little more pocket change, a little
Rambo to kick the shit out of the whodunit
my anger is stewing, it is crowding me
like a mannequin presented purposely
for lightning and other impulsive
natures, how the weather accrues to make
us more solipsistic, don't want to carry any kind
of roots around and only speak to my brothers
feeling akin to a generation of westerners beating-up
affiances, when we came into our own I was afraid
having wanted to hide and pretend to be another woman
to throw away all my clothes and reinvent a
new theory, a theory of feathers and warrior
gear, a theory pronounced she-warrior
with a tad bit of neo-punk but I am
nothing, having nothing to invent or be
extraordinary about and while reading
the introduction to an 1844 novel
it said how writing was *awesome*
I thought, what more could you ask for—

Acknowledgements

Some of these poems were included in a chapbook *DIGITAL MACRAMÉ* published by Poor Claudia in Portland, Oregon. My biggest thanks to Drew Scott Swenhaugen and Marshall Lee Walker.

Special thanks to the editors of these journals who originally published versions of some of these poems: *So and So Magazine; Forklift, Ohio; Notnostrums; Jubilat; Softblow; LIT Magazine; Conduit; Ilk Journal; Sprung Formal; Interrupture; TRNSFR Mag; Paradigm Magazine; TheThePoetry; Sixth Finch; Death Hums;* and *NAP*. Poems from this collection also appear in the anthology *Language Lessons: Volume I* (Third Man Books 2014).

I would also like to thank my loving poet-in-crime Sampson Starkweather, for being an editor, friend, and companion; Elaine Kahn, who has made me the poet that I am, and some of my dearest friends who have been distinctly supportive: Ben Mirov, Amy Lawless, Jackie Clark, Julia Cohen, Christie Ann Reynolds, Lauren Hunter, Ben Pease, Bianca Stone, Eric Amling, Dan Magers, Chris Tonelli, Justin Marks, Dan Boehl, Farrah Field, Jared White, Emily Pettit, Guy Pettit, Cynthia Arrieu-King, Brett Price, and Brenda Iijima.

Thanks to my publisher Megan Burns for believing in this book and for putting it out into the world. Thank you to Jovah Mclemore for the beautiful cover design. Thanks Sommer Browning, Brandon Downing, Rachel B. Glaser, Filip Marinovich, & Frank Sherlock for your encouragement and super rad language.

Always the hugest of love to my family!

The following poems are respectfully dedicated to these individuals:
Your Wing Deck is a Lazy Beetle is for Emily Pettit
Blanket the Storm is for Dan Boehl
I Can't Stand Behind You is for Justin Marks
Not For June is for Julia Cohen

This book is for you and you and you...

Paige Taggart is a Northern Californian and currently resides in Brooklyn. *Want for Lion* is her first full-length collection. Her second book *Or Replica* will be published by Brooklyn Arts Press. She is the author of 5 chapbooks: *Last Difficult Gardens* (Horse Less Press), *DIGITAL MACRAMÉ* (Poor Claudia) *Polaroid Parade* (Greying Ghost) and *The Ice Poems* (DoubleCross Press), and forthcoming *I am Writing To You From Another Country; Translations of Henri Michaux* (Greying Ghost Press). She earned her MFA from the New School and was a 2009 NYFA fellow. She works as a full-time jewelry production manager & additionally makes her own jewelry (mactaggartjewelry.com)

Advance Praise for *Want for Lion*

What is the difference between expression and, well, there is nothing else. The question, like Taggart's book, plots against itself. Maybe it's a set up, a Möbius strip of language. Or maybe it's a window into a world governed by a truer anti-logic where "litter is literally glittering," where poetry is always "kinda screamed." Her voice is Scarface and titties cloaked in the syntax of study and propelled by a roaring heart.
- **Sommer Browning**

Taggart's poems sulk, prance, and attack like a beast she's tamed into her house cat. Nature is the beauty and danger beating behind each line. Taggart holds and waves a flag of honesty at every house party, emotional journey, and private moments, illuminating and obscuring the parts familiar to us all.
- **Rachel B. Glaser**

There's a persistent sensation in *Want for Lion* of being yoked to a mind in full stream. It's faster than you. It foams in a forest of registers. There is work to be done as a reader to reach this new speed: stumbling, knees ripped, I think I have. "I want to make people feel so small that they think I'm the sky," says the Poet. I'm here to tell you that's exactly what happens.
- **Brandon Downing**

Paige Taggart punctures identity papers with inky harpoon ritual, process in every line, gone beyond epiphany package. She is a poet who dares to value attention over status when most poems read like elaborate status updates. Her rhythm shakes me out of screen trance into a labyrinth of the gloriously unfixable self.
- **Filip Marinovich**

Paige Taggart's *Want for Lion* is an earth goddess journal that is divine text & scandal sheet, reaching through/across our surfaces with detoxified beauty & the eye of Hecate's owl. Hymns & dirges score the transmorphic in layered registers, *tracking some reformed species* that resembles ours, desperately in need of re-forming. This book is a *chariot pick-me-up*, w/ invocations of sweet dreams & the nightmares we just might deserve. Some blessings go unrealized until they're held in the hands. You are holding one now.
- **Frank Sherlock**

Titles from Trembling Pillow Press

I of the Storm by Bill Lavender

Olympia Street by Michael Ford

Ethereal Avalanche by Gina Ferrara

Transfixion by Bill Lavender

The Ethics of Sleep by Bernadette Mayer

Downtown by Lee Meitzen Grue

SONG OF PRAISE Homage To John Coltrane by John Sinclair

Untitled Writings From A Member of the Blank Generation by Philip Good

DESERT JOURNAL by ruth weiss

Aesthesia Balderdash by Kim Vodicka

Of Love & Capital by Christopher Rizzo (Winner of the 2012 Bob Kaufman Book Prize selected by Bernadette Mayer)

SUPER NATURAL by Tracey McTague

I LOVE THIS AMERICAN WAY OF LIFE by Brett Evans

Q by Bill Lavender

loaded arc by Laura Goldstein

Psalms for Dogs and Sorcerers by Jen Coleman (Winner of the 2013 Bob Kaufman Award selected by Dara Wier)

Want for Lion by Paige Taggart

Forthcoming Titles

Trick Rider by Jen Tynes

Website: http://www.tremblingpillowpress.com

www.ingramcontent.com/pod-product-compliance
Lightning Source LLC
Chambersburg PA
CBHW022115090426
42743CB00008B/860